MUSIC THEORY

Grades 1 - 5
IN A NUTSHELL

Maureen Cox

First published 2001
by **Subject Publications**
  Bishops Court
  Broadstone
  Dorset BH18 8NF

ISBN 1 898771 17 0

From the sale of this book the Author
and Publishers will make a donation to
The Beethoven Fund For Deaf Children
(Charity Registration no. 282844).

Printed by Pardy & Son (Printers) Ltd.,
Parkside, Ringwood, Hampshire, BH24 3SF
Tel: +44 (0)1425 471433
Fax: +44 (0)1425 478923

For my husband

★ ★ ★ ★ ★ ★

This book is for anyone who is learning to sing or play a musical instrument and who is studying the theory of music.

You can look up key signatures, major and minor scales, intervals, ornaments and instruments of the orchestra. You will also find help with writing rhythms and composing melodies. Two sections at the end of the book cover the essential musical signs and the key French, German and Italian words needed for Grades 1 to 5.

This book is an extremely useful revision aid as well as being an invaluable reference source that you will find fun to use.

★ ★ ★ ★ ★ ★

I am grateful to the many Professional Private Music Teachers and Schools who use Theory is Fun with their pupils and who have encouraged me to produce this reference book.

Maureen Cox

CONTENTS

Notes and Rests

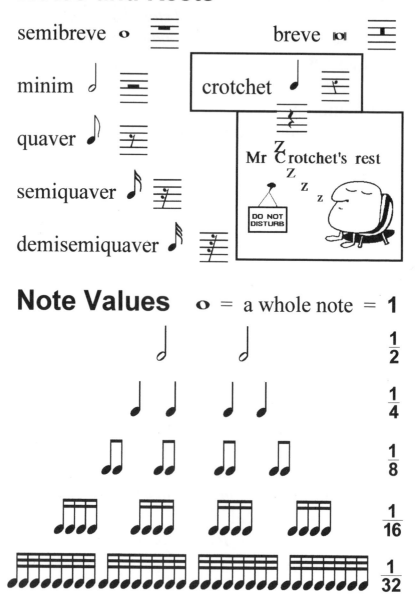

semibreve

minim

quaver

semiquaver

demisemiquaver

breve

crotchet

Mr Crotchet's rest

DO NOT DISTURB

Note Values

o = a whole note = **1**

		$\frac{1}{2}$
		$\frac{1}{4}$
		$\frac{1}{8}$
		$\frac{1}{16}$
		$\frac{1}{32}$

Dotted Notes

Single Dot

A dot after a note is worth **half** the value of the note.

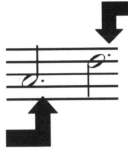

A dot is placed in the **same space** if a dotted note is **in a space**.

A dot is placed in the **space above** if the dotted note is **on a line**.

Double Dot

A single dot after a note lengthens it by half.	The second dot is worth half the first dot.
𝅗𝅥· = 𝅗𝅥 + ♩ ♩· = ♩ + ♪	𝅗𝅥·· = 𝅗𝅥 + ♩ + ♪ ♩·· = ♩ + ♪· + ♪

Duplets

The duplet is found in **compound time**
$\frac{6}{4}$, $\frac{6}{8}$, $\frac{9}{4}$, $\frac{9}{8}$ etc., when a **dotted beat** is
divided into **2 equal parts**.

There are two ways of writing the duplet:-

1. Using dotted notes	2. Using a **2** above the pair of notes

Triplets

A triplet is a *group of three* equal value
notes or a group of three equal value notes
and rests, *played in the time of two*.

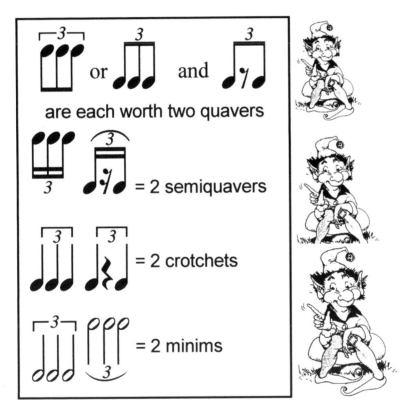

are each worth two quavers

= 2 semiquavers

= 2 crotchets

= 2 minims

*NB. For repeating triplets, the bracket and
the number 3 may sometimes be omitted!*

Time Signatures

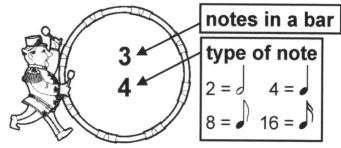

notes in a bar

type of note

$2 = \half$ $4 = \quarter$

$8 = \eighth$ $16 = \sixteenth$

Simple Time

duple		$\frac{2}{4}$	¢ or $\frac{2}{2}$
triple	$\frac{3}{8}$	$\frac{3}{4}$	$\frac{3}{2}$
quadruple	$\frac{4}{8}$	C or $\frac{4}{4}$	$\frac{4}{2}$

Compound Time

duple	$\frac{6}{16}$	$\frac{6}{8}$	$\frac{6}{4}$
triple	$\frac{9}{16}$	$\frac{9}{8}$	$\frac{9}{4}$
quadruple	$\frac{12}{16}$	$\frac{12}{8}$	$\frac{12}{4}$

Irregular Time

quintuple	$\frac{5}{8}$	$\frac{5}{4}$	
septuple	$\frac{7}{8}$	$\frac{7}{4}$	

Anacrusis

last bar

+ = one complete bar

Beaming Notes

In a group of beamed notes the stems all go up or all go down.

If notes are beamed, the furthest note from the middle line has the correct stem.

middle line

Grouping Notes and Rests

You must group together notes and rests to show clearly the rhythm of the music.

Simple Time

1. Beam *quavers* in a *whole bar* of duple or triple time.

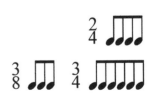

2. Beam *half a bar of quavers* for beats 1 & 2 or 3 & 4 *but never* 2 & 3 in quadruple time.

3. Beam *in beats* notes *less* than a *quaver* in $\frac{2}{4}$ time.

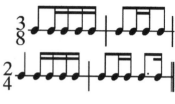

4. Beam *quavers* and *semiquavers* into crotchet beats.

5. Beam together *semiquavers* if allowed.

6. Beam *demisemiquavers* together as *whole* or *half* beats.

7. Beam a group of four quavers if you could replace them by a minim.

8. Beam a group of four semiquavers if you could replace them by a crotchet.

9. Try to avoid tied notes. Use a semibreve rather than a tied minim if possible but *never* join beats 2 & 3.

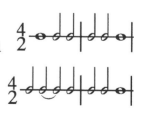

10. For a **_whole bar's rest_** use a **_breve rest_** in $\frac{4}{2}$ time. Use a **_semibreve rest_** in every other time signature.

11. In duple and triple time give each beat its own rest.

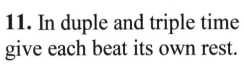

12. In quadruple time, use a single rest to join beats 1 & 2 or 3 & 4 but **_never_** beats 2 & 3.

Compound Time

1. Group notes into **_whole beats_**. Remember that **a whole beat is always a dotted note.**

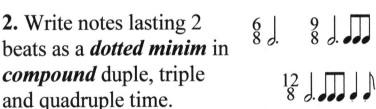

2. Write notes lasting 2 beats as a **_dotted minim_** in **_compound_** duple, triple and quadruple time.

3. For a **_whole bar_** in $\frac{9}{8}$ time write a dotted minim tied to a dotted crotchet.

4. For a ***whole bar*** in $\frac{12}{8}$ time write a dotted semibreve.

5. The rules for rests in compound time are the same in simple time but remember **a whole beat is a dotted note!**

6. Use rests to join quavers 1 & 2 but not 2 & 3 of a dotted crotchet.

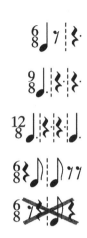

Irregular Time Signatures

13. Group notes in quintuple time, in combinations of two or three beats [2+3] or [3+2].

14. Group notes in septuple time, in combinations of two or three beats [4+3], [3+4], [2+2+3], [2+3+2] or [3+2+2].

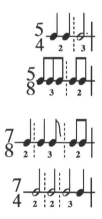

Irregular Time Divisions

A group of 5, 6 or 7 notes can be given the
same time value as a group of 4 notes and

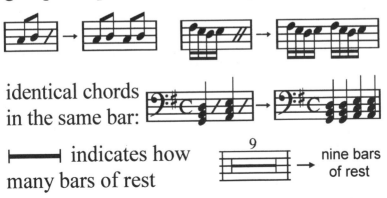

a group of 9 notes as a group of 8 notes.

Repetition of Notes and Rests

✦ and ✦ indicate repeating notes:

groups of quavers and semiquavers:

identical chords
in the same bar:

▬▬▬ indicates how
many bars of rest

9
——→ nine bars
of rest

Tones and Semitones

There is a **semitone** between B & C and E & F because there is no black key between them on a keyboard.

Every step between a **black** and **white** key is **one semitone**. There are **two semitones** in **one tone**.

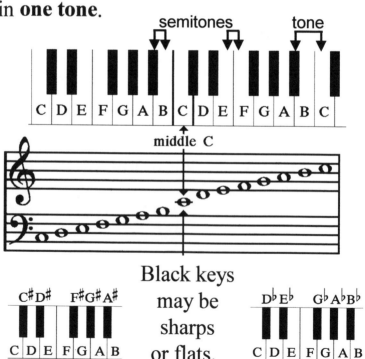

Black keys may be sharps or flats.

Keyboard and Clefs

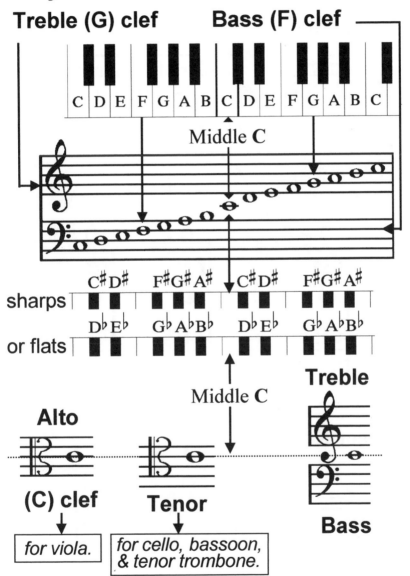

Key Signatures - Sharps

Major Keys

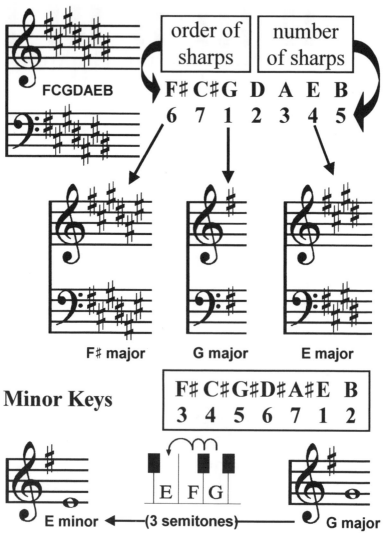

order of sharps	number of sharps

FCGDAEB

F♯ C♯ G D A E B
6 7 1 2 3 4 5

F♯ major   G major   E major

Minor Keys

F♯	C♯	G♯	D♯	A♯	E	B
3	4	5	6	7	1	2

E minor ◄—(3 semitones)—— G major

E F G

Key Signatures - Flats

Major Keys

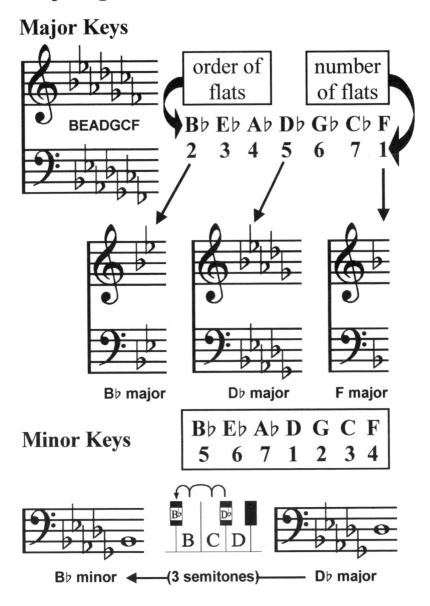

order of flats

number of flats

BEADGCF

B♭	E♭	A♭	D♭	G♭	C♭	F
2	3	4	5	6	7	1

B♭ major   D♭ major   F major

Minor Keys

B♭	E♭	A♭	D	G	C	F
5	6	7	1	2	3	4

B♭ minor ◄——(3 semitones)—— D♭ major

page 19

Major Scales

The pattern of **Tones** and **Semitones** is **T T S T T T S** with a semitone between notes 3 & 4 and between notes 7 & 8.

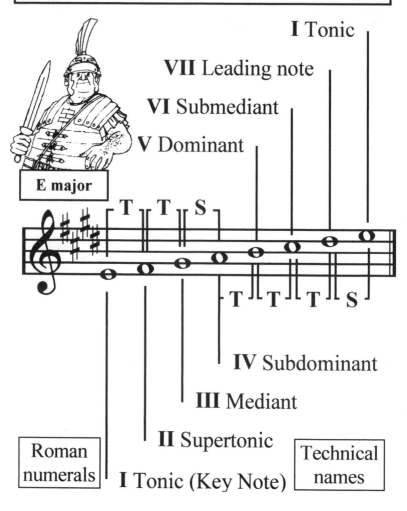

I Tonic

VII Leading note

VI Submediant

V Dominant

E major

T T S

T T T S

IV Subdominant

III Mediant

II Supertonic

Roman numerals

I Tonic (Key Note)

Technical names

Minor Scales

All minor scales have

- a semitone between notes 2&3

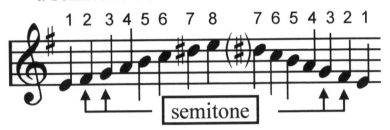

semitone

- accidentals - not in the key signature:

sharp (♯) - raises note 1 semitone

double sharp (×) - raises note 2 semitones

natural (♮) - restores note to original pitch

 NB ♮♯ - restores note to original pitch
     then raises note one semitone

flat (♭) - lowers note 1 semitone

double flat (♭♭) - lowers note 2 semitones

 NB ♮♭ - restores note to original pitch
     then lowers note one semitone

Harmonic minor scales

- are the **same** ascending and descending
- have 1 semitone between notes 2&3 and 5&6

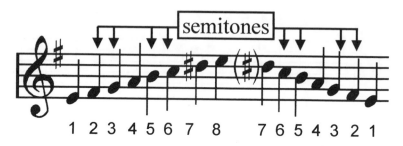

- have 3 semitones between notes 6&7

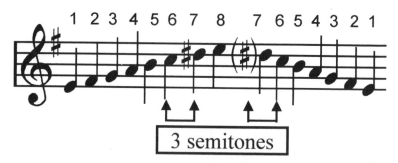

Melodic minor scales

- are **different** ascending and descending
- have one semitone between notes 2&3
- notes 6&7 are **raised** 1 semitone ascending and **lowered** 1 semitone descending

- have **one** semitone between notes 7&8 *ascending* and **two** semitones (1 tone) *descending*

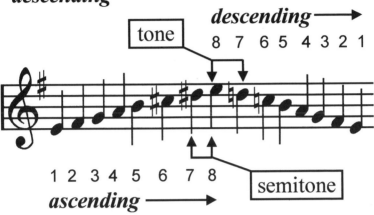

- have one **tone** between 5&6 *ascending* and one **semitone** *descending*
- have **one tone** between notes 6&7 ascending ***and*** descending

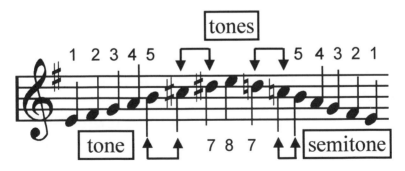

Chromatic Scales

A chromatic scale is a thirteen note scale composed entirely of semitones.

To write a harmonic chromatic scale

1. Put the key-note at both ends.

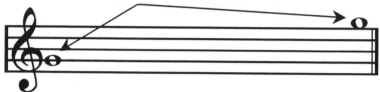

2. Write the dominant once only.

3. Put *two* notes on all the other lines and in all the other spaces.

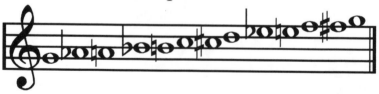

Construction of the chromatic scale is identical for the major and minor key both ascending and descending.

Major Scales and their Relative Harmonic Minor Scales

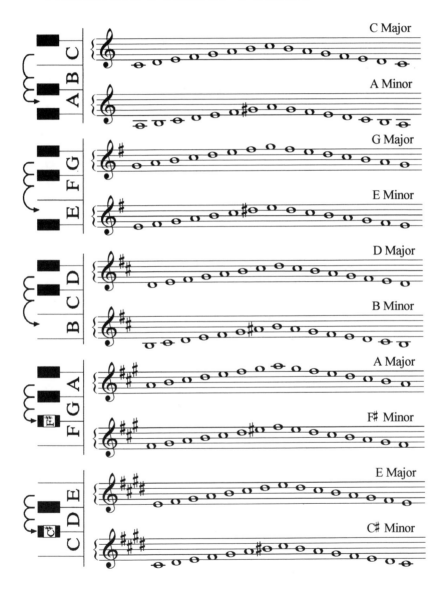

N.B. Enharmonic notes have the same pitch but different names: e.g. F sharp and G flat.

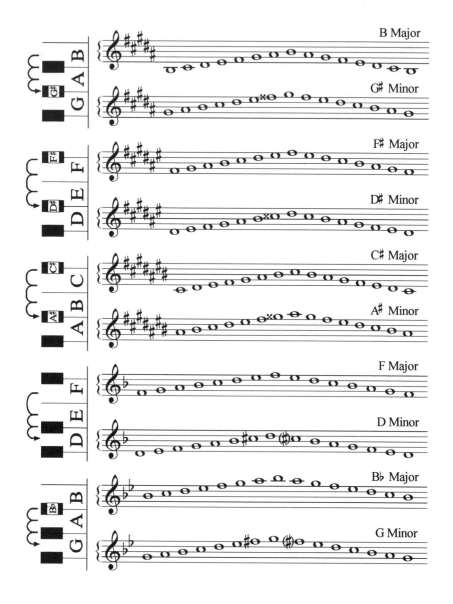

N.B. Enharmonic minor scales: G# & A♭; E♭ & D#; major scales: D♭ & C#; B# & C♭; F# & G♭.

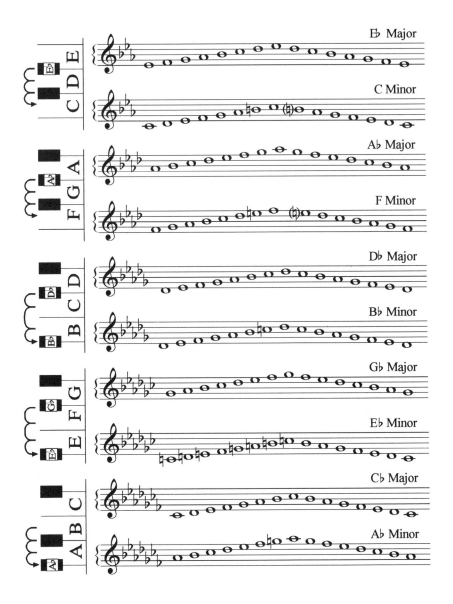

Melodic Minor Scales

The 6th & 7th notes raised when ascending and then lowered again when descending.

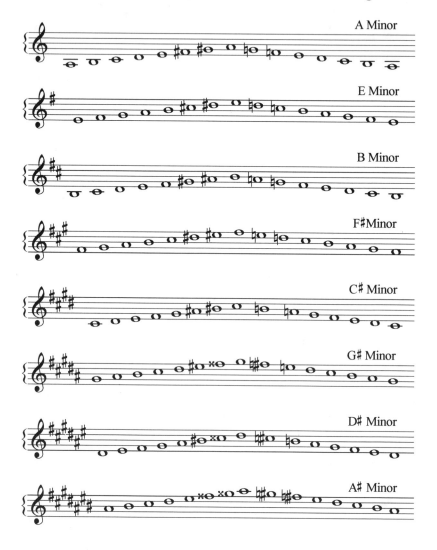

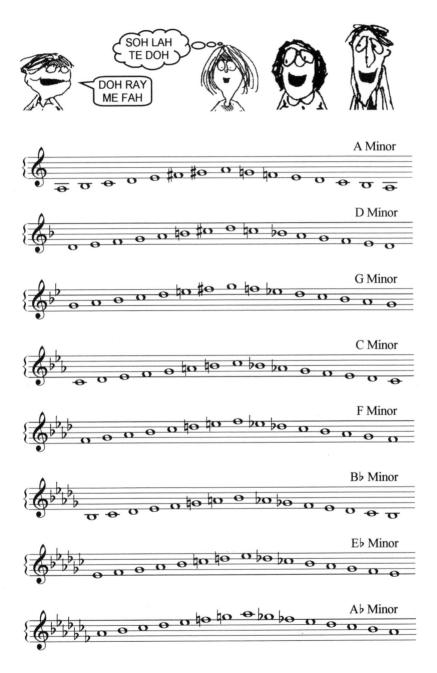

Intervals

An interval is the difference in pitch between two notes.

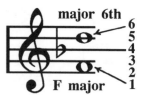

Scales		Name of Interval		Number of Semitones
Major	**Minor**			
Octave (Perf.8th)		Perfect	8th	12
Major 7th	Minor 7th	Augmented	7th	12
		Major	7th	11
		Minor	7th	11
		Diminished	7th	9
Major 6th	Minor 6th	Augmented	6th	10
		Major	6th	9
		Minor	6th	8
		Diminished	6th	7
Perfect 5th		Augmented	5th	8
		Perfect	5th	7
		Diminished	5th	6
Perfect 4th		Augmented	4th	6
		Perfect	4th	5
		Diminished	4th	4
Major 3rd	Minor 3rd	Augmented	3rd	5
		Major	3rd	4
		Minor	3rd	3
		Diminished	3rd	2
Major 2nd		Augmented	2nd	3
		Major	2nd	2
		Minor	2nd	1
		Diminished	2nd	-

Augmented Interval

 one semitone **more** than a **major** interval or **perfect** interval.

Diminished Interval

 one semitone **less** than a **minor** interval and two **less** than a **major** interval.

Compound Interval

 an interval **greater** than a **perfect 8th** or **octave**. A *compound* 2nd, 3rd, 4th, 5th, etc., is also called a 9th, 10th, 11th, 12th.

Harmonic Interval

 two notes written one above the other and played at the same time.

Melodic Interval

 two notes written one after the other and played separately.

Chords

two or more notes played
at the same time (see also
intervals on pages 30-31)

Triad

chord of three notes
root, third (3rd) and fifth (5th)
refer to the notes of a triad

Primary Triads

triads formed on the first [tonic (I)], fourth
[subdominant (IV)] and fifth [dominant (V)]
notes (degrees) of a scale

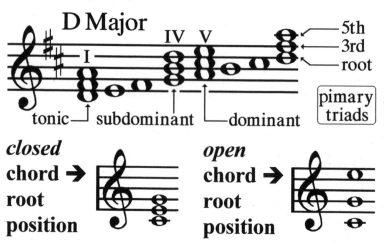

D Major

I   IV V

5th
3rd
root

tonic   subdominant   dominant

pimary triads

closed
chord →
root
position

open
chord →
root
position

Inversions

triads can be written
in three positions

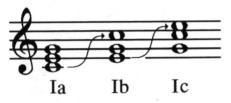

Ia   Ib   Ic

(a) root position

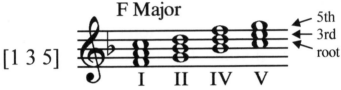

[1 3 5]   F Major   ← 5th ← 3rd ← root   I II IV V

(b) first inversion

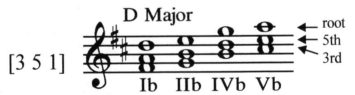

[3 5 1]   D Major   ← root ← 5th ← 3rd   Ib IIb IVb Vb

(c) second inversion

[5 1 3]   A Major   ← 3rd ← root ← 5th   Ic IIc IVc Vc

Cadences

a cadence consists of two chords

Perfect Cadence [V+I]

dominant chord followed by tonic chord

leading note → tonic in the treble
dominant → tonic in the bass

Imperfect Cadence [I+V *or* II+V *or* IV+V]

any chord followed by dominant chord

Plagal Cadence [IV+I]

subdominant chord
followed by
the tonic chord

Ornaments

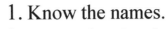

1. Know the names.
2. Recognise the signs.
3. Know how to play them.

Acciaccatura

played as quickly as possible on the beat,
just before playing the main note

also called a *short grace note* and not to be
confused with an appoggiatura

[*Italian:* acciaccare – squeeze in]

Appoggiatura ♪

Double 🎵 and Triple 🎵

Grace note value depends on the main note.

two-thirds when the *main note* is *dotted*

one-half when the *main note* is **not** dotted

[*Italian:* appoggiare – lean against]

Arpeggio 🎵

ripple the notes
from bottom to top so that
each note of the chord
is played in turn and held.

[*Italian:* arpeggiare – play harpwise]

Upper Mordent ∿

three notes - main note, the note *above* and then the main note - played as quickly as possible in the time of the main note

Inverted or Lower Mordent ∿

three notes - main note, the note *below* and then the main note - played as quickly as possible in the time of the main note

Mordent with Accidental

the accidental applies to the *middle* note and is written *above* the upper mordent sign and *below* the lower mordent sign

Upper Turn ∾
and Inverted or Lower Turn ⮌

may be written *above* or *after* a note

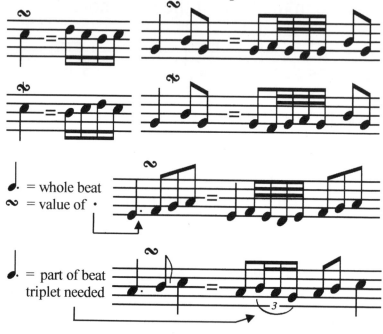

J. = whole beat
∾ = value of ·

J. = part of beat
triplet needed

A Turn with Accidentals

an accidental may be written
above and *below* the sign
indicating to which note
the accidental applies

Trill or Shake *tr* 〰〰

played with the *note* and the *note above*

early composers
eg. Bach

modern composers
eg. Dvorak

start trill on the
upper note

start trill on the
principal note

grace note
begins trill

start trill on
upper note

include in the trill
any *grace notes*

avoid repeated notes at the start
and end of a trill by adding, if
necessary, an extra note and
introducing a triplet

Instruments of the Orchestra

Concert Pitch

pitch at which we hear an instrument

For some instruments, concert pitch is *lower* than the *written notes* in their music.

instrument	*note written*	*note played*
clarinet in B♭ trumpet in B♭	C	B♭
clarinet in A cornet in A trumpet in A	C	A
cor anglais French horn	C	F

Clefs

treble   alto   tenor   bass

Clef Chart for Orchestral Instruments

	instrument	treble	alto	tenor	bass
strings	violin	●			
	viola		●		
	cello			●	●
	double bass				●
	harp	●			●
woodwind	flute	●			
	piccolo	●			
	oboe	●			
	cor anglais	●			
	bassoon			●	●
	double bassoon				●
	clarinet	●			
	saxophone	●			
brass	trumpet	●			
	horn	●			●
	trombone			●	●
	tuba				●
percussion	timpani				●
	tubular bells	●			
	vibraphone	●			
	xylophone	●			
	glockenspiel	●			
	piano	●			●

Strings

each stringed instrument has a range of about 3½ octaves and can play two strings at the same time

string quartet = trio + 1 violin
string quintet = quartet + 1 viola or cello

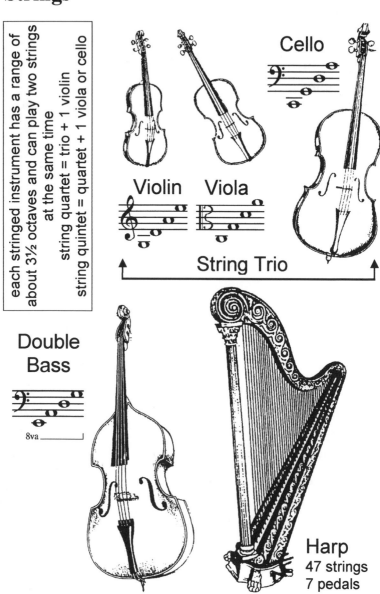

Cello

Violin   Viola

String Trio

Double Bass

8va

Harp
47 strings
7 pedals

Woodwind

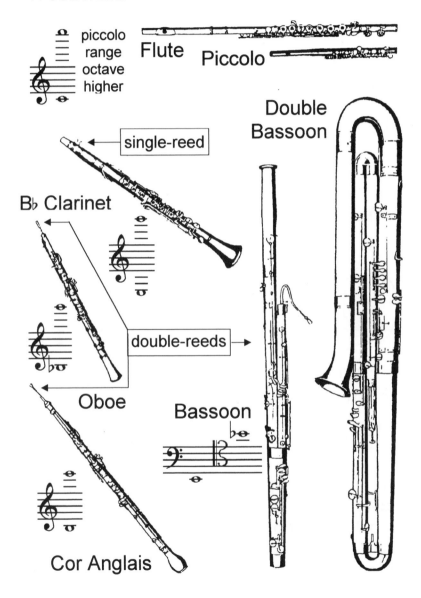

piccolo
range
octave
higher

Flute   Piccolo

single-reed

B♭ Clarinet

Double
Bassoon

double-reeds

Oboe

Bassoon

Cor Anglais

Brass

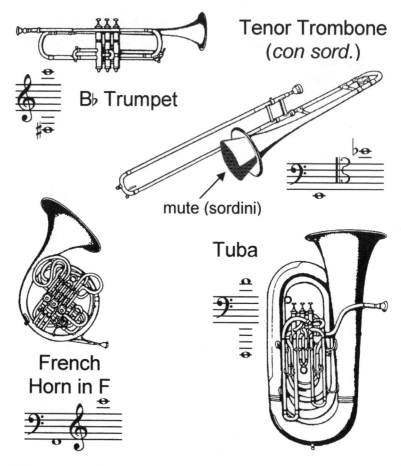

Tenor Trombone
(*con sord.*)

B♭ Trumpet

mute (sordini)

Tuba

French
Horn in F

The sounds are produced by vibration of the players lips. The pitch of the note is changed by pulling in or pushing out the slide of the trombone or by opening and closing the valves of the trumpet, horn and tuba.

Percussion

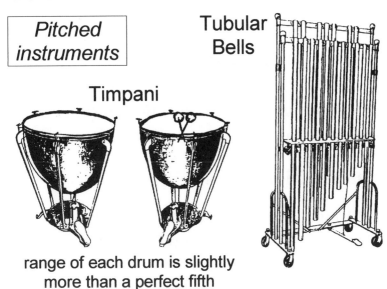

Pitched
instruments

Tubular
Bells

Timpani

range of each drum is slightly
more than a perfect fifth

Glockenspiel, vibraphone and xylophone
are also *pitched* percussion instruments.

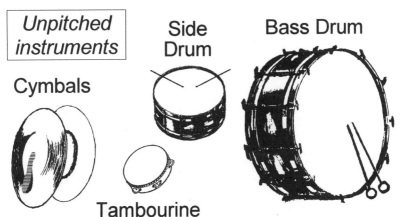

Unpitched
instruments

Side
Drum

Bass Drum

Cymbals

Tambourine

Transposition

A change in the key of a piece of music by raising or lowering the pitch of notes by a given interval. Major 2nd, minor 3rd, perfect 5th and octave are the intervals used by transposing orchestral instruments.

Transposition Rules

1. a major key transposes to a major key and a minor key → a minor key.

transpose down by one octave

C major → C major

transpose up by one octave

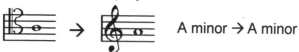

A minor → A minor

2. for odd-numbered intervals, 3rd, 5th, etc., notes on lines → notes on lines and notes in spaces → notes in spaces.

up a minor 3rd
E major → G major

down a perfect 5th
F# minor → B minor

3. for even-numbered intervals, 8va, 2nd, etc., notes on lines → notes in spaces and notes in spaces → notes on lines.

down a major 2nd
G major → F major

up a major 2nd
C minor → D minor

4. for a piece, with accidentals, transposed to include the new key signature, any notes with an accidental → notes with an accidental.

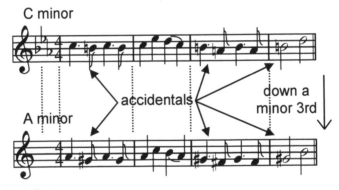

Handy Hints:

  1. line up the key signatures, time signatures and bar-lines.

  2. when the interval is an octave, check that transposed note has the same letter name as the original note.

Voices in Score

Soprano, Alto, Tenor and Bass are the voices in four-part choral music. Each of these voices has an approximate range.

Composing a Short Melody

When composing an eight-bar melody for an instrument or fitting words to music, ***begin with the rhythm!***

Two, Four and Eight-bar Rhythms

- check or choose the time signature
- write the notes on a single line
- obey the rules for grouping notes and rests

anacrusis – *an opening starting before 1st beat of bar 1*

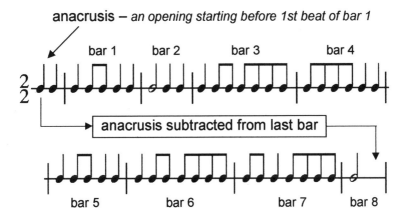

anacrusis subtracted from last bar

- tap out loud the rhythms in strict time
- experiment with different rhythms
- do not end a rhythm with a semiquaver

- write 4-bar phrases, with the rhythm of the last two bars answering the rhythm of the first two bars of a phrase

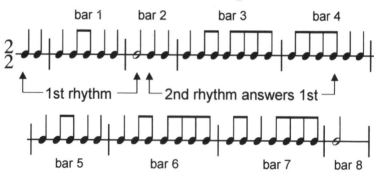

Bars 1 & 5 are the same and bars 3 & 6 are the same

- repeat rhythms to help bind the four bars and the two phrases together
- end on a strong beat
- aim to write the rhythm for an 8-bar melody as two phrases of four bars each

Writing a Rhythm to Words

When writing a rhythm to fit words, ***read them carefully to determine the mood!***

We three Kings of Orient are
Bearing gifts we traverse afar
Field and fountain, moor and mountain,
Following yonder star.

- put bar-lines in front of important syllables

| We three Kings of | Orient are
| Bearing gifts we | traverse afar
| Field and fountain, | moor and mountain,
| Following yonder | star.

- choose a time signature, fit a note to each syllable and then group the notes
- remember that compound duple, triple and quadruple time signatures allow you to divide a beat into three

We three Kings of O - ri - ent are   Bear - ing gifts we   tra - verse a - far

Field and foun - tain, moor and mou - n - tain, Fol - low - ing yon - der star.

Eight-bar Melody for an Instrument

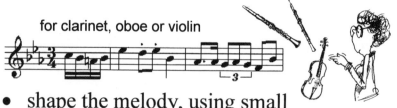

for clarinet, oboe or violin

- shape the melody, using small ascents and descents
- move upwards in the first four bars to reach the highest note, usually from the dominant chord.
- move downwards to the final note, often the tonic
- avoid awkward intervals, keeping to scale and broken chord movements
- add performance directions - tempo, dynamics and phrasing marks

Setting Words to Music

The Northwind doth blow and we shall have snow.
What will poor Robin do then, poor thing?
He'll go to a barn and keep himself warm, and
hide his head under his wing, poor thing!

- read the words and compose the
  rhythm to capture the mood

- select a key and compose a melody,
  keeping within a range of a 12th
- add performance directions - tempo,
  dynamics and phrasing marks

Musical Terms

A (à) - at, to, by, for, in the style of
  A tempo - resume the normal speed
Aber - but
Accelerando - becoming gradually faster
Adagietto - rather slow
Adagio - slow, leisurely
Adagissimo - very slow
Ad libitum; **ad lib.** - at choice; play freely
Affetuoso - tenderly
Affrettando - hurrying
Agitato - agitated
Alla - in the style of
  Alla marcia - in the style of a march
  Alla polacca - in the style of a Polonaise
Allargando - broadening out
Allegretto - slightly slower than allegro
Allegro - lively, reasonably fast
  Allegro assai - very quick
Amabile - amiable, pleasant
Amore - love
Andante - at a walking pace
Andantino - a little slower or
    a little faster than andante
Anima - soul, spirit

Animato - lively, animated
Animé - animated, lively
Appassionata - with passion
Arco - play with the bow
Assai - very
Assez - enough, sufficiently
Attacca - go on immediately
Ausdruck - expression
Avec - with
Baritone - voice between bass and tenor
Ben - well
Bewegt - with movement. agitated
Bravura - with boldness and spirit
Breit - broad, expansive
Brillante - sparkling, brilliant

Calando - getting softer, dying away
Cantabile - in a singing style
Cantando - in a singing style
Cédez - yield, relax the speed
Col; **Con** - with
Come - as
    Come prima - as before
    Come sopra - as above
Con anima - with deep feeling - soul
Con brio - with vigour
Con moto - with movement

Con sordini - play with a mute
Con spirito - with spirit, life, energy
Crescendo [cresc.] - gradually louder
Da capo [D.C.] - from the beginning
Dal segno [D.S.] - repeat from the sign [𝄋]
Deciso - with determination
Decrescendo [decresc.] - gradually softer
Delicato - delicately
Diminuendo [dim.] - gradually softer
Dolce - sweetly
Dolcissimo - very sweetly
Dolente - sadly
Dolore - grief, sorrow
Doppio - double
Doppio movimento - double the speed
Douce - sweet
E; ed - and
Ein - a, one
Einfach - simple
En dehors - prominent
Energico - with energy
Espressione - expression
Espressivo [Espress., Espr.]
   - with expression, feeling
Estinto - as soft as possible, lifeless
Et - and

Etwas - somewhat, rather
Facile - easy
Fortepiano [fp] - loud, then immediately soft
Fine - the end
Forte [f] - loud
Fortissimo [ff] - very loud
Forza - force, power
Forzando [fz] - with a strong accent
Fröhlich - cheerful, joyful
Fuoco - fire

Furioso - furiously
Giocoso - merry
Giusto - exact, proper
Grandioso - in a grand manner
Grave - very slow
Grazioso - gracefully
Immer - always
Incalzando - getting quicker
Lacrimoso - tearfully
Langsam - slow
Largamente - in a broad style
Larghetto - faster than largo
Largo - slow & stately, broad
Lebhaft - lively
Legatissimo - as smoothly as possible
Legato - smoothly

Légèrement - lightly

Leggiero - lightly

Lent - slow

Lento - slowly

L'Istesso - the same

Loco - at the normal pitch (cancels 8va)

Lunga - long

    Lunga pausa - long pause

Lusingando - coaxing

Ma - but

Ma non troppo - but not too much

Maestoso - majestically

Mais - but

Marcato, marc. - marked, accented

    Ben marcato - well marked

Martellato - hammered out

Marziale - in a military style

Mässig - at a moderate speed

Meno - less

Meno mosso - less movement

Mesto - sadly

Mezzo forte [mf] - moderately loud

Mezzo piano [mp] - moderately soft

Mezzo-soprano - voice between alto and soprano

Misterioso - mysteriously

Misura - measure
    Alla misura - in strict time
    Senza misura - in free time
Mit - with
Moderato - at a moderate pace
Modéré - at a moderate speed
Moins - less
Motto - much
Morendo - dying away
Mosso - movement
Moto - movement
Movimento - movement

Nicht - not
Niente - nothing
Nobilmente - nobly
Non - not
Non tanto - not so much
Non troppo - not too much
Ohne - without
Ossia - or
Parlando - in a speaking manner
Parlante - in a speaking manner
Pastorale - in a pastoral style
Patetico - with feeling
Perdendosi - dying away
Pesante - heavily

Peu - little
Piacevole - plaintive
Pianissimo [pp] - very soft
Piano [p] - soft
Più - more
Pizzicato [pizz.] - plucked
Plus - more
Pochettino; poch. - rather little
Poco - a little
    Poco a poco - little by little
Possibile - possible
Presto possibile - as fast as possible
Presser - hurry
    En pressant - hurrying on
Prestissimo - as fast as possible
Presto - very quick
Prima, primo - first
Prima volta - first time
Quasi - as if, resembling
Ralentir - slow down
Rallentando [rall.] - becoming gradually slower
Retenu - held back
    En retenant - holding back
Rinforzando; [rf., rfz.] - reinforcing
Risoluto - boldly
Ritardando [ritard., rit.] - gradually slower

Ritenuto [riten., rit.] - hold back, slower at once
Ritmico - rhythmically
Ruhig - peaceful Sans - without
Scherzando, scherzoso – playfully, joking
Scherzo - a joke
Schnell - fast
Seconda, secondo - second
    Seconda volta - second time
Segno - sign [𝄋]
Segue - go straight on
Sehr - very
Semplice - simple
Sempre - always
Senza - without
Senza sordini - without a mute
Sforzando [sf, sfz] - with a sudden accent
Simile [Sim.] - in the same way
Slargando - gradually slower
Slentando - gradually slower
Smorzando [smorz.] - dying away
Sonoro - with rich tone
Sopra - above
Sospirando - sighing
Sostenuto - sustained
Sotto - below
Sotto voce - in an undertone

Spiritoso - lively, animated
Staccatissimo - very detached
Staccato - short, detached
Stringendo - gradually faster
Subito - suddenly
Sul G - play on the G string
Sul ponticello - play near the bridge
Suss - sweet
Tanto - so much
Tempo - speed, time
Tempo comodo - at a comfortable speed
Tempo primo - resume the original speed
Tempo rubato - with some freedom of time
Teneramente, tenerezza - tenderly, tenderness
Tenuto - held on
Tosto - swift, rapid
Tranquillo - quietly
Traurig - sad
Très - very
Triste, Tristamente - sad, sorrowful
Troppo - too much
Tutti - all
Un, une - one
Und - and
Veloce - swift
Vibrato - vibrating

Vif; Vite – lively, quick
Vivace, Vivo - lively, quick
Vivacissimo - very lively
Voce - voice
Volante – flying, fast
Voll - full
Volta - time
Volti subito [V.S.] - turn the page quickly

Wenig - little
Wieder - again
Zart - tender, delicate
Zu - to, too

Musical Signs

 - accent, slightly separating note

 - accent and strongly accent note

 - pause on the note

 - semi-staccato

 - staccato [short, detached]

 - super-staccato [staccatissimo]

 - tie or bind same notes together

V   ⊓.   - bow up and bow down

⎯⎯⎯◁   - becoming louder

▷⎯⎯⎯   - becoming softer

◁▷   - becoming louder then softer

‖: :‖   - start repeat and end repeat

♩ = 60   - 60 crotchet beats in a minute

⌢   - slurs: play the group of notes smoothly as one phrase

8va ⎯⎯⎯⎤
8 - - - - - - ⎦   - play an octave higher

8va ⎯⎯⎯⎦
8 - - - - - - ⎦   - play an octave lower

♪   ♪   - acciaccatura and appoggiatura

♯   ×   - sharp and double sharp

∽   ⸫   - turn and inverted turn

∿   ∿   - upper and lower mordent

tr ∿∿∿   - trill or shake

⸾   - arpeggio (harp-like)

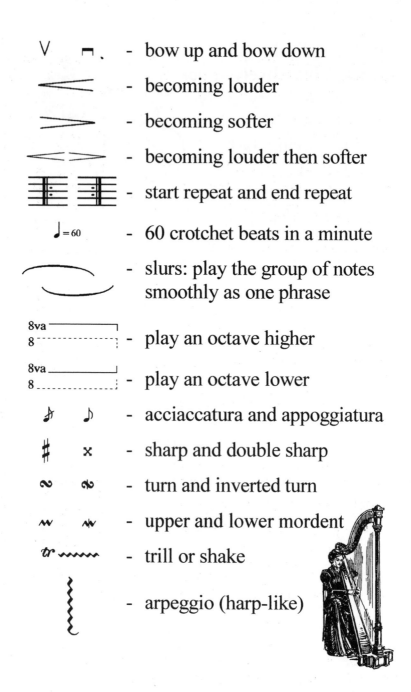